THE MARGE BOOK

THE SIMPSONS™ LIBRARY OF WISDOM
THE MARGE BOOK

HarperCollins Publishers,
10 East 53rd Street, New York, NY 10022.
FIRST EDITION
ISBN 978-0-06-169880-4

09 10 11 12 13 SC 10 9 8 7 6 5 4 3 2 1

Publisher: Matt Groening
Creative Director: Bill Morrison
Managing Editor: Terry Delegeane
Director of Operations: Robert Zaugh
Art Director: Nathan Kane
Special Projects Art Director: Serban Cristescu
Production Manager: Christopher Ungar
Assistant Art Director: Chia-Hsien Jason Ho
Production/Design: Karen Bates, Nathan Hamill, Art Villanueva
Staff Artist: Mike Rote
Administration: Sherri Smith, Pete Benson
Legal Guardian: Susan A. Grode

THE SIMPSONS™ LIBRARY OF WISDOM

Conceived and Edited by Bill Morrison
Book Design, Art Direction, and Production by Serban Cristescu
Contributing Editor: Terry Delegeane

HarperCollins Editors: Hope Innelli and Jeremy Cesarec

Contributing Artists:
KAREN BATES, JOHN COSTANZA,
SERBAN CRISTESCU, DAN DAVIS, MIKE DECARLO, ISTVAN MAJOROS,
SCOTT MCRAE, BILL MORRISON, KIMBERLY NARSETE, KEVIN M. NEWMAN,
MIKE ROTE, ROBERT STANLEY, ERICK TRAN

Contributing Writers:
MARY TRAINOR, SCOTT M. GIMPLE

Special Thanks to:
N. Vyolet Diaz, Deanna MacLellan, Helio Salvatierra, Mili Smythe, and Ursula Wendel

THE MARGE BOOK

Maggie

HARPER

NEW YORK • LONDON • TORONTO • SYDNEY

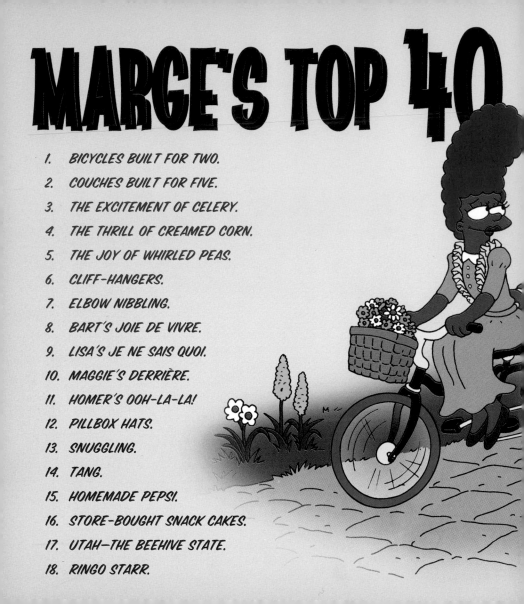

MARGE'S TOP 40

1. BICYCLES BUILT FOR TWO.

2. COUCHES BUILT FOR FIVE.

3. THE EXCITEMENT OF CELERY.

4. THE THRILL OF CREAMED CORN.

5. THE JOY OF WHIRLED PEAS.

6. CLIFF-HANGERS.

7. ELBOW NIBBLING.

8. BART'S JOIE DE VIVRE.

9. LISA'S JE NE SAIS QUOI.

10. MAGGIE'S DERRIÈRE.

11. HOMER'S OOH-LA-LA!

12. PILLBOX HATS.

13. SNUGGLING.

14. TANG.

15. HOMEMADE PEPSI.

16. STORE-BOUGHT SNACK CAKES.

17. UTAH—THE BEEHIVE STATE.

18. RINGO STARR.

MARGE'S DAILY LOG

TUESDAY

6:30 AM: Homie's alarm clock goes off. I wake up, while Homer hits the snooze button for the first of seven times.

6:45 AM: Make breakfast for the family: Rock Candy-Os for Bart, mashed organic spelt for Lisa, and a pureed banana for Maggie.

7:00 AM: Walk Bart and Lisa to the bus stop. On the way, I make Bart promise to get through the day without any tomfoolery, shenanigans, or monkey business.

7:30 AM: Send Homie to work with an Egg McHomie sandwich-to-go in a full-body bib, put Maggie in her baby swing, turn on her Baby Feinstein Piano DVD, and take a shower.

7:45 AM to 8:45 AM: Dry hair.

9:15 AM: Stop at Stockpilers Food Warehouse Club for the essentials. Breakfast on free samples.

11:00 AM: Load the car. I strap the 400 ct. "Wetty Bye-Bye" Diaper package to the roof and break up juice box cases to properly distribute weight throughout car.

12:00 PM: Make Maggie lunch. Have a lunch of Melba toast, Melba peaches, and wonder whatever happened to Melba Moore.

12:30 PM: Begin my daily cleaning routine, including: dusting the moldings, whitening the bathroom grout, lampshade swiffering, and degumming under Bart's place at the table.

3:00 PM: Get a call from Springfield Elementary. Bart has turned Principal Skinner's office into an aviary using peanut butter and birdseed and opening all the windows. I tell them it's impossible because Bart promised me he wouldn't engage in any tomfoolery, shenanigans, or monkey business. They classified it as a "caper."

4:00 PM: While Lisa does her homework, I send Bart to his room and show my anger with my best disapproving murmur and start the Whatsamatta U Enchilada Stew I found in "The Jay Ward Cookbook."

5:30 PM: Homer gets home from work, and I tell him what Bart did. He marches into Bart's room, and pretty soon I hear him and Bart having a "dueling burps" contest.

6:00 PM: Dinner. No one compliments what I made, but their crazed gorging is thanks enough.

7:00 PM: Bart surprises me by washing and drying the dishes. I hug him and cry for four whole minutes. (I know because Bart times it using the microwave clock.) I say a silent prayer that my guilt will be enough to put my son on the straight and narrow, or at least keep him one step ahead of the authorities.

8:00 PM: The family watches "Cagefighting With the Stars" together. Say what you will about Elisabeth Hasselbeck, but that petite thing is scrappy!

9:00 PM: Homer puts Maggie and Bart to bed while I read to Lisa from "A Brief History of Time" by Stephen Hawking. At one point, I see the entire universe for what it is: a complex, achingly beautiful cosmic machine, fueled by both math and miracles...and then I realize it's just the enchilada stew backing up.

9:48 PM: Homie and I snuggle on the couch and I realize that he has fallen asleep and I'm wedged between him and the couch.

10:34 PM: Finally, a fast food commercial for "Krusty's Pre-Dunked Donut Holes" wakes Homer, and I'm free. Homer vows to get up on time tomorrow so he can stop at Krusty Burger.

11:04 PM: I set Homer's alarm clock to go off an hour earlier so he'll have time to get the donut holes before work. I'll be up an hour earlier, but that's sixty more minutes I get with Al Roker!

11:30 PM: I say my prayers and pray for my family, my country, my world, and a good new Meg Ryan movie. I look up at the moldings, and they're clean as a whistle. It's been a good day.

A Brief History of the
Bouvier Women

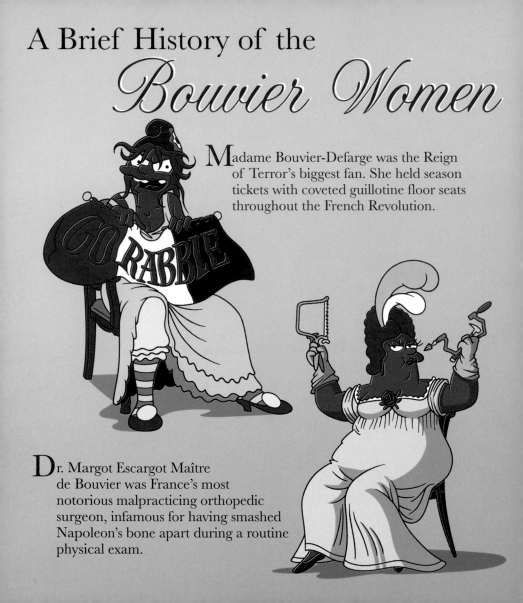

Madame Bouvier-Defarge was the Reign of Terror's biggest fan. She held season tickets with coveted guillotine floor seats throughout the French Revolution.

Dr. Margot Escargot Maître de Bouvier was France's most notorious malpracticing orthopedic surgeon, infamous for having smashed Napoleon's bone apart during a routine physical exam.

Ennui Bouvier was the founder of the Belle Époque's school of Expressionlessism—a listless style of painting characterized by Ennui as, "So What? Who Cares?"

Bebe Bebe Bouvier Déjà Vu was the first woman to compete in the Tour de France. Being extremely modest, Bebe Bebe insisted on riding her bicycle sidesaddle, and thus came in dead last.

Fifi Bouvier Au Jus was a stubborn, cantankerous woman who became a symbol of the French Resistance when she refused to move her Citroën out of the way as the Wehrmacht marched into Paris.

Brigitte Bidet Bouvier was a dancer at the popular Dijon Poupon A-Go-Go, birthplace of such famous European dance crazes as the Hokey Le Pokey, the Mashed Potatoes au Gratin, and Le Urquél.

Edwina "Big Eddie" Bouvier and Edwina "Little Eddie" Bouvier became cult figures after the 1975 documentary film *Gray Garters* showed the mother and daughter living in squalor in a decrepit mansion in Springfield's Recluse Ranch Estates.

Jacqueline Ingrid Gurney Bouvier is the widow of Clancy Bouvier, who was one of the earliest male flight attendants.

Patty Bouvier is the only openly lesbian Bouvier, although rumors did swirl around Ennui Bouvier in her lifetime. As always, Ennui simply said, "So what? Who cares?"

Selma Bouvier-Terwilliger-Hutz-McClure-Simpson is considered to be the most married Bouvier, having out-husbanded the late Genevieve Bouvier-Papier-Mâché-Macramé by one husband.

Marge Bouvier Simpson is famous for her marshmallow squares.

Though Marge tells her family that she loves them an average of every 3.1 hours, she does things well above and beyond the maternal call of duty to show Homer and the kids just how special they are to her! Here are just a few of

The Special Little Ways Marge Tells 'em She Loves 'em!

1. Makes realistic-looking ribs out of tofu, pretzel rods, and beet juice so Lisa doesn't feel left out at barbecues.

THEY IMPLODED THE OUR LADY OF PERPETUAL SORROWS CONVENT TODAY—THE ONE THAT OLD NUN CARVED WITH JUST A SPOON AND FAITH!

BLOWUPS, BRINGDOWNS, & TAKEDOWNS

2. Videotapes televised building implosions and police chases for Homer and Bart.

3. Always keeps an emergency supply of binkies she's "broken in" for Maggie.

4. Buys and wraps Christmas presents for the kids to give to Homer.

5. Buys and wraps Christmas presents for Homer to give to the kids.

6. Buys and wraps Christmas presents for the kids and Homer to give to her.

7. Irons the pages of Lisa's schoolbooks for extra crispness.

8. Always makes surplus snacking dough when baking cookies.

9. Edits down episodes of "Jeopardy!" so they only feature questions about Grand Funk Railroad, alcohol, and sandwiches so Homer can feel smart.

10. Always keeps papier mâché volcano materials on hand for last-minute science projects.

FIRST CALLED BY ITS CURRENT NAME IN 1878, THIS SQUARE, ORANGE CHEESE IS SOLD IN PACKAGES OF 18 AND 36 SLICES.

11. Regularly drives out of state to pick up Extra-Chunky Duff Peanut Butter Lager, Homer's favorite beer that's been discontinued in the state Springfield is in.

12. Actually wears a Tooth Fairy costume when collecting teeth under pillows, just in case the kids wake up.

13. Triple-frosts all the kids' birthday cakes and quadruple-frosts Homer's.

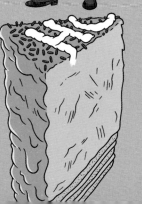

MARGE'S HOUSEHOLD HELPERS

2 Hours of Hammock Time — Expires 12-22-08 Not Valid with other offers

1) Roll Some Gutter Balls! Tape homemade coupons ("Good for One Favorite Meal," "Good for Four Hours of Uninterrupted Television," "Good for One Nag-Free Weekend") to tennis balls and throw them on the roof, along with Twinkies, bowling passes, and sports blooper DVDs. Soon, your hubby will be chomping at the bit to get at those gutters!

2) Get Sporty! Set up a scoreboard, a timer, and a hoop with a backboard to throw debris through, and make cleaning out gutters a sport unto itself. Get together with other wives or life companions on the block and form a league!

3) Fair Trade! Give your husband a plastic bag when he goes up to the roof—tell him whatever gunk he frees from the gutters, you'll match its weight in cookies, pie, chili, or his favorite meat dish.

4) Get Your Guilt On! Right before your husband gets home, make it look like you've fallen off the ladder trying to clean the gutters yourself. When your husband sees you and rushes over, try to get to your feet, saying, "I'm fine. I just felt like cleaning the gutters. Don't mind me..." Consider crying. Even after a hard day of work, it's entirely possible your husband will clean the gutters right then and there. He may even buy you dinner!

Husband to Clean the Gutters!

5) Create a Stairway to Heaven!

Make the ladder your husband's favorite place! Outfit it with a sound system to blast Hank Williams Jr.'s "Are You Ready for Some Football?," install a video monitor for watching action movies, put hot water foot massagers on every rung, and keep a fully stocked basket of water balloons near the top!

6) Fear Is Your Friend! Leave newspaper clippings about how standing water in gutters is a haven for West Nile-laden mosquito larvae, how gutter ice kills over 150 people every year, and how unkempt gutters help attract gangs and other criminals to once-peaceful neighborhoods. Amp up the terror, and soon your gutters will be sparkling!

These stages reflect a variety of reactions that may surface as an individual spouse struggles to cope with his or her plight. Expressing and accepting all these feelings is an important part of the numbing process known as marriage.

HOPE   ACCEPTANCE   HUMILIATION   REVENGE   DENIAL

REGRET   SHOCK   PITY   HYSTERIA   HORROR

TALES TORN FROM THE HEART OF SPRINGFIELD

The Secret Life of Homer's Wife

KISS ME, MY DARLING! A KISS THAT WILL LAST ME ALL THROUGH MY DRAB AND DREARY DAY!

*E*VERY HOUSEWIFE IN AMERICA KNOWS THE FEELING...YOUR LOVING HUSBAND GOES OFF TO WORK, YOUR ADORABLE CHILDREN HEAD FOR SCHOOL... AND THEN, OFF IN THE DISTANCE, YOU HEAR THE STEADY HUM-DRUMMING OF THE HUMDRUM...

HOW I LONGED TO HAVE A LIFE BEYOND THESE INTERIOR LATEX-PAINTED WALLS.

:SIGH.:

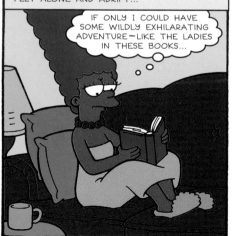

LATER THAT AFTERNOON, AS I CURLED UP ON THE SOFA WITH A ROMANCE NOVEL, I FELT ALONE AND ADRIFT...

IF ONLY I COULD HAVE SOME WILDLY EXHILARATING ADVENTURE—LIKE THE LADIES IN THESE BOOKS...

WHEN SUDDENLY, THE DELIGHTFUL SOUND OF WOMEN'S LAUGHTER FLOATED INTO MY CHAMBER OF SOLITUDE...

TEE HEE HEE!

HAR DE HAR HAR!

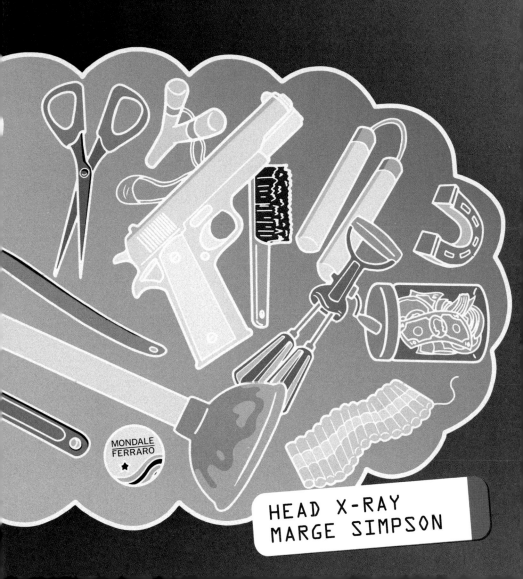

HEAD X-RAY
MARGE SIMPSON

MONDALE
FERRARO
★

Mama's Daytime

	2:00 PM	2:30 PM
OOH!	**THE OPAL SHOW** Yakking.	**THE V.U.** Yammering.
YIKES!	**THESE OLD LEFTOVERS** Host Bob Beeler restores some of America's oldest food.	**PIMP MY BRIDE** Spouse remodel.
hey!	**LOCKE & LODE** *(Crime Drama)* Detectives Locke and Lode undergo plastic surgery to boost sagging ratings.	
EEK!	**THE BOLD AND THE SANS SERIF** *(Soap Opera)* Property values plummet when a family of Italics moves in next door.	
GASP!	**ONE DAY AT A TIME OF OUR LIFE TO LIVE** *(Soap Opera)*	**YOUNG REPUBLICANS** *(Soap Opera)*
EWW	**MOVIE: A CHILD IS BORED** *(Tragedy)* Based on the true story of a young girl growing up in suburbia with nothing to do.	
SPIT	**ONE AND A HALF LAFFS** *(Sitcom)*	**TWO'S COMPANY** *(Sitcom)*
¡EH!	**¿DÓNDE ESTÁ EL BAÑO?** *(Discusión)*	**¿QUÉ?** *(Close-Captioned)*

Dramas TV LISTINGS

3:00 PM	3:30 PM
HARD HAIRBALL WITH ITCHY & SCRATCHY Mindless punditry and violence.	**SMELLS LIKE SPRINGFIELD** Nosing around with Kent Brockman.

MOVIE: BRINGING UP PHLEGM *(Screwball Comedy)*
Hijinks ensue when a madcap heiress comes down with pulmonary tuberculosis.

CHARLIE'S AGENTS
Charlie's numerous calls to his agents via speakerphone go unreturned.

THE IMMATURE AND THE HYPERACTIVE *(Soap Opera)* Jason, Julie, and Josh confront Jessica, Justin, and Jesse about Jordan and Jennifer.

JUDGE CONSTANCE HARM *(Courtroom Drama)* Judge Harm throws the book at a man caught stealing from the public library.

AFTER SCHOOL BUMMER: OMIGOD! PLEASE, DAD! NO! A young girl's father dresses like a 'tard.

THREE'S A CROWD *(Sitcom)*	**ENOUGH'S ENOUGH** *(Sitcom)*
SEÑOR DING-DONG *(Telenovela)*	**¡NO ME GUSTA!** *(Obras de Jabón)*

CANYONERO'S EXCLUSIVE EXHIBITIONIST PACKAGE COMES EQUIPPED WITH ALL THESE SELF-AGGRANDIZING FEATURES THAT YOU'LL NEVER USE:

Brush Guard! • Ski Lift! • Rooftop Swivel Turret! • Midrange Assault Water Nozzle! • Deep Sea Anchor! • Adjustable Bazooka Mount!

Fuel-Efficient – Self-immolating 72-gallon gas tank backed by our "explode-on-impact-or-your-money-back guarantee."

Seating – Up to 35 comfortably/ 42 excruciatingly.

Picnic-ready – 16-ton cargo hold!

For the ladies! Be sure to check out the female-friendly **F-Series:** Complete line of upholstery-matching shoes and handbags! Lipstick lighter and special nail polish drying side vents.

For the guys! Steak-scented interior (not available in the F-series)

Reverse-Sensing Audio System – Drowns out any unpleasant crashing sounds or screams when you back over a neighbor's fence or spouse.

SEE FOR YOURSELF WHY THE CANYONERO IS CALLED

the Cadillac of Automobiles

PAYMENT GUESSTIMATOR

Here's a quick, simple way to estimate the purchase or lease cost of your new Canyonero:

[Your Weekly Take-Home Pay] X [Recommended PSI Tire Pressure] = Monthly Payment.

How to Get Your

1) Make it happen with marketing! How can vegetables compete with the big food companies' branded candy, cereal, mascots, and sugary yogurts? Well, do what they do! Take veggies you prepare for your kids and put them in homemade, brightly colored plastic wrappers with flashy logos and cute cartoon mascots you draw yourself!

2) Unleash the Godzilla within! Create tiny innocent villagers out of veggies! Your child won't be able to keep themselves from biting their wholesome, nutritious heads off!

3) Get 'em veggie-zealous by getting 'em jealous! Buy a rabbit and favor it over your child every time it eats a carrot.

Kids to Eat Their Veggies!

4) Sneak attack when they get a snack attack! Replace the peanuts in Snickers® bars with celery and green peppers! (This takes practice!) Alternate the candy with jicama cubes in PEZ® dispensers! Use food dye to color soybeans and stick them in bags of M&M's®!

5) Have your cake (and veggies) and eat 'em, too!
Serve carrot cake that's 90% carrot and 10% cake.

6) Pile it on! Remember, as a child, the fun of burying yourself in a leaf pile after raking? Re-create that feeling and encourage vegetable eating by putting your kids on a tarp and burying them in salad, slaw, or simply kale! (Tidiness Tip: Don't use dressing.)

★ SPRAWL

"If WE don't have it,

IN OUR PRODUCE SECTION

GORILLA'S CHOICE BRAND
BANANAS

69¢ LB.
GET YOUR OPPOSABLE THUMBS
ON A BUNCH TODAY!

FARM-WILTED
LETTUCE

39¢ LB.

SOUR
GRAPES

$2.99 LB.

MACINTOSH
APPLES

99¢ EACH
(DOWNLOAD NOW)

CARCASS OF VALUES MEAT DEPT.

UTILITY GRADE
PORK BUTTOCKS
$3.39 LB.

ENGLISH SADDLE-CUT
HORSE CHOPS
$4.19 LB.

U.S.D.A.
SUBPRIME
Carcass of Values
Satisfaction Guaranteed

USDA SUBPRIME
SIDE-SPLIT
RIB TICKLERS
$4.69 LB.

USDA SUBPRIME
GRISTLE-FILLED
MEAT THINGIES
$2.39 FISTFUL

-MART ★

YOU don't need it!"

-MART ★

AFTER-SCHOOL TREAT

CRYSTAL BUZZ COLA

12-LITER ATTENTION-DEFICIT HYPERACTIVE SIZE

$8.99

CHAIRMAN MEOW'S CHINESE CAT FOOD

FORTIFIED WITH MELAMINE!

5 FOR $2 (6-OZ. CANS)

UNLEASH THE AWESOME POWER OF APPLES!

POWERSAUCE BARS

4 FOR $5

IRISH DITCH BODY WASH

8-GAL. DRUM

2 FOR $12

NATURE'S SHAME
BLADDER PADS

2 FOR $8

AT SPRAWL-MART WE KNOW HOW IMPORTANT BUYING A CARTLOAD OF CRAP IS TO YOU AND YOUR FAMILY. THAT'S WHY WE SELL ONLY THE CHEAPEST GOODS IN THE BIGGEST POSSIBLE BULK CONTAINERS. OUR DRAFTY, CAVERNOUS WAREHOUSE STORES ALLOW US TO SAVE ON FLOORING, FURNISHINGS, AND HEATING BILLS. THAT MEANS WE CAN TURN THOSE SAVINGS INTO HIGHER PROFITS AND PASS THEM ALONG TO OUR CEO.

TALES TORN FROM THE HEART OF SPRINGFIELD

The Secret Life of Homer's Wife

LET THERE NEVER, EVER BE ANY SECRETS BETWEEN US, MARGE! NEVER! EVER! UNLESS, OF COURSE, THERE'S SOMETHING ONE OF US DOESN'T WANT THE OTHER ONE TO KNOW.

BUT I DID HAVE A SECRET: I WAS A BORED, DISCONTENTED HOUSEWIFE. I ACHED TO ADD SOME SORT OF EXCITING, MEANINGFUL ACTIVITY TO MY DAY, BUT I HAD NO IDEA HOW TO GO ABOUT IT...

THEN, ONE DAY WHILE SHOPPING AT BOOKACHINOS...

WHY, MARGE SIMPSON! I COULDN'T HELP BUT NOTICE YOU BROWSING THE *STEAMY PAPERBACK ROMANCE* SECTION...

OH! HELLO, RUTH.

LADIES LITERATURE

I'M LOOKING FOR A REPLACEMENT COPY OF MISS BRONTÉ'S *JANE EYREHEAD*... THE DOG CHEWED UP THE LAST 244 PAGES BEFORE I HAD A CHANCE TO REACH THE SATISFYING CONCLUSION.

JANE EYREHEAD

JEAN COCTEAU'S LES ENFANTS TERRIBLES

OOOH. GOTHIC NOVELS WITH HEADSTRONG, YET SENSITIVE, BYRONIC HEROES. "MAD, BAD, AND DANGEROUS TO KNOW..." EH, MARGE?

WELL, ACTUALLY I LIKE THE PARTS ABOUT PENNILESS ORPHANS FINALLY GETTING A NICE, HOT MEAL.

BENJAMIN SPOCK'S THE COMMON SENSE BOOK OF BABY AND CHILDCARE

MMM. DON'T WE ALL? YOU KNOW, YOU SURPRISE ME, HONEY.

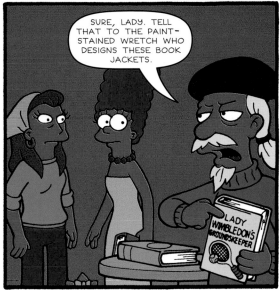

I WAS WALKING ON AIR! IMAGINE...RUTH POWERS ASKING *ME* TO JOIN THE ULTRA-COSMOPOLITAN JET-SETTERS IN HER SOPHISTICATED LADIES BOOK CLUB! MY DARK DAYS AS A FRUSTRATED HOUSEWIFE WERE OVER!

Rip My Bodice!

MARGE'S LASCIVIOUS LIBRARY OF UNBRIDLED ROMANCE NOVELS

- Lady Ashblush's Unladylike Grip
- THE LUSTY PLOWMAN'S PROGRESS
- THE VIRILE COACHMAN'S CARRIAGE OF DESIRE
- THE EXCEEDINGLY IMPUDENT FOOTMAN
- RAVAGED BY PASSION'S PURPLE PROSE
- The Strapping Tradesman's All-Purpose Tool
- EXPLORING SQUIRE REDBLOOD'S VAST ACREAGE
- Miss Starchy's Forbidden Drawers
- A Most Bothersome Corset
- The Lieutenant's Sword Unsheathed
- THE VULGAR CANDLESTICK MAKER

The Secret of the Vicar's Knickers

THE LAIRD OF THROBBYN CASTLE

A MAN CALLED MANLY

Replenishing the Butler's Pantry

Plumping His Mistress's Mattresses

Saddling Her Ladyship's Equestrian Mount

The Mystery of the Manor Woman

THE ICE COLD PITCHER OF WOO

THE ROYAL POSTMAN'S CUMBERSOME PACKAGE

Lord Beefcake's Blushing Chambermaid

THE BEASTLY CAD'S STICKY WICKET

HAY FERVOR: A Stable Boy's Coming of Age

The Constable's Odd Query

The Fishmonger's Codpiece Unbound

Her Sea Captain's Navel Command

Unbuckle My Swash!

THE 24 TYPES OF MOTHERS

The Fear-Mongering
Suburban Vigilante

The Nearly
Invisible Woman

The Happy Homewrecker

The Gin-Swilling
Recovering Alcoholic

The Free-Spirited
What-the-Heller

The Melodramatic
Guilt Tripper

YOU MEET AT THE PTA

The Glamorous
Go-Getting Career Gal

The Swinging Divorcée

The Loudmouthed
Emotional Damage-Doer

The Life-Sucking
Soul Killer

The Vaguely Dissatisfied
Happy Homemaker

The World's Greatest
#1 Top Mom

The Ruthless
Social Climber

The Widow Maker

The Systematic
Self-Esteem Squasher

The Cruel and
Unusual Disciplinarian

The Finger-Pointing
Blame Shifter

The Tight-Assed
Trophy Mom

The Mother/Sister/
Cousin/Niece

The Fast-Tracking
Child-Free Executrix

The Shameless Hussy

The Ego-Destroying
Control Freak

The Octuplet-Wrangling
Super-Breeder

The Pantywaisted
Mr. Mom

maggiesmom

Bloggin' 'n' Braggin' 'bout

ACTION ITEMS

The Three T's
What to do when your days are filled with Teething, Toddling, and Tantrums.
READ/POST COMMENTS

Out of Baby Food?
Don't panic—here's a list of yummy blender-friendly leftovers you're sure to find in your fridge.
READ/POST COMMENTS

Feeling Pesticidal
When my fourth-grader brought home head lice last week, I felt angry and ashamed.
READ/POST COMMENTS

My Baby, Myself
I am she and she am me and we are all together, coochie-coochie-coo.
READ/POST COMMENTS

None Dare Call It Day Carelessness!
My hard-hitting exposé of the Ayn Rand School for Tots.
READ/POST COMMENTS

LOL MAGGIE

I CAN HAS PACIFIZER?

I STOLE MOMMY'S HEART
WHAT R U IN FOR?

I'M IN UR CATBOX
PWNING UR SAND.

OMG I POOPIE IN THE TUB!

A PIECE OF MARGE'S MIND

Don't get me started about those so-called leak-proof diapers!
READ/POST COMMENTS

I am so irked at PBS for canceling the Baby Edward Teller show!
READ/POST COMMENTS

.com

SEARCH

MY BABY

MAGGIE ALERT
Up-to-the-minute Account of
Acts of *Acute* Adorableness
> SIGN UP

I CAN'T HEAR MYSELF TYPE
LIVE BLOGGING FROM WALL E. WEASEL

WHAT WE'RE SPITTING OUT THIS WEEK:

Creamed Corn Paste

Butternut Squashed Turnips

Peas and Pork Rinds

Broccoli and Liverwurst

Pureed Banana Skins

**Surplus Army and
Navy Beans**

Chicken Noodle Nuggets

Strained Gruel

LINKS BY CATEGORY
Snuggly Wugglies
Tootsie Wootsies
Honey Bunnies
Tickly Tummies
Cuddly Cutsies
Huggie Buggies
Namby Pambies

MOMMY BLOG LINKS
From the Diaper Pail
Harvard or Bust!
Passing Remarks about
Other People's Children
Nap Time Is Martini Time
Goo Goo Google
Mommy's Had It up to Here
Claiming the Child Tax Credit on
Form 1040

LATEST POLL RESULTS

**Our Mommies Online
Cutest Baby poll ended
in a 2,462-way tie with
everybody's baby getting
one vote each.**

TODAY'S FALL DOWN GO BOOM COUNT

How to Get Your Kids to Play Outside!

1) Acclimate them to actual climate! It's happened a few times—things have gotten really busy (for example, dealing with the litigation against my husband after he ate a prize-winning butter statue) and my kids have gone months without playing outside. When that happens, I like to reintroduce my kids to "the wild" by setting up the living room in the backyard. The simple act of watching TV and playing video games in the fresh air is a great first step toward actual outdoor play.

2) Remote Control! Shaking that TV addiction is nearly impossible—so make it work for you! Hide the TV remote somewhere in the neighborhood and tell them they have an hour to find it or it will be "terminated." Watch those little junkies run!

3) Have your dog take your kid on a walk! A) Use leash to tie child to dog. B) Cook some bacon. C) Tie bacon to bike. D) Go for ride; dog runs after bike; kid runs after dog.

4) Make the outdoors a hit! Your kids will spend hours outside with the proper motivation! Once a week, I have my kids put on weight belts, I give them yardsticks, and then I hang a piñata—just out of reach—filled with marshmallow fluff and quarters!

5) Get 'em movin' for movies! What's the ultimate indoor activity? Going to the movies! Offer to take your kids to a film they want to see more than ANYTHING. Wait about twenty minutes before showtime and then tell them you won't be taking the car to get there.

6) Scare 'em into sunlight! Before your kids come home from school hide a few boomboxes around the house set to play creepy sound effects CDs, whip up some fake blood, block off some vents to make some areas of the house particularly cold, and have your neighbors dress up as poltergeists. When the little ones get home and park themselves in front of the boob tube, regretfully inform them that you've discovered the house was built on top of an Indian burial ground that was later the site of a horrible ice cream truck accident. Then, let the fearsomeness fly! With the right kind of scares, you can make your home a forlorn place of abject horror that your kids won't want to spend a moment in!

7) Send 'em six feet under! Every child has a prized possession: a teddy bear, a blanket, an action figure, or, for an unpopular child, a stuffed raccoon. A great way to get that child outside and active is to bury that beloved object deep in the backyard!

VIVA LA VINYL!

Heavy Hits from Marge's Record Collection

The Fantastic Jefferson Electric Bagel

Psychedelicatessen

Major Chutney's Bleeding Hearts Club Orchestra - Greatest Hit

Jackson Denver - Songs of a Self-Absorbed Cowboy

Men without Pants - The Underwear Dance

The Larry Davis Experience - Live at Springfield Prison

The Fantastic Jefferson Electric Bagel - Psychedelicatessen

Buffalo Bruce Springfield - A Brand New Jersey

Footdance - Motion Picture Soundtrack

The Motown 5 – I Just Called to Say Baby, Baby, Baby, Baby, Oh, Baby

The Sex Lawyers – Never Mind the Bollocks, Stop Infringing on My Copyrights

The Surf Boys – Sun of a Beach

John Coyote Melonhead – A Truckload of Pickup Commercials

Spandex – Stretch This Disco

The Stewardesses – Unfasten Your Seat Belt

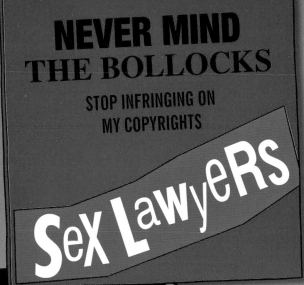

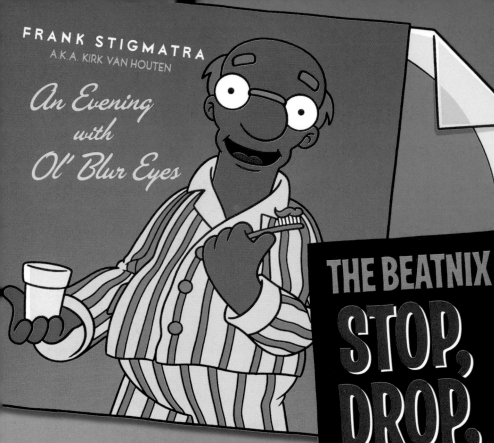

FRANK STIGMATRA
A.K.A. KIRK VAN HOUTEN

An Evening with Ol' Blur Eyes

Frank Stigmatra –
An Evening with Ol' Blur Eyes

Joanie Twitchell – What I Had for Breakfast

Barbra Stressman – Just Me and My Ego

Will E. Neilson – Tie a Big Bandana
'Round My Sweaty Ol' Head

THE BEATNIX

STOP, DROP, and BOP

Mopeche à la Mode – Super-Synthesize Me

The Beatnix – Stop, Drop, and Bop

It Takes a Village, People –
Saturday Night Flu

Squirmin' Hawkins – Do the Squirm!

AbbaZabba – Home Swede Home

Willie and the Weasels –
Me Luv's in the Loo

Turn Your Head

The Tailgater

The Republican's Wife

The Fairer Faucet

The Braidy Bunch

The Bow Must Go On

The Eight-Tease

and *Coif!*

A DOZEN DELIGHTFUL TRUE-BLUE DO'S

The Right On, Sister

The Big Flipper

The Nervous Breakdown

The Mummy's Curse

The Rasta Blasta

The Marge

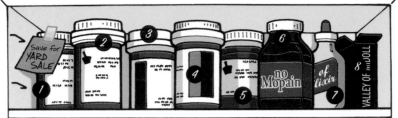

Let's Take a Look Inside
MARGE'S MEDICINE CABINET

1. Zowhat™ Pre-traumatic Stress Relief
2. HooKares™ Mood Brightener
3. WottEvah™ Gloom and Despair Reducer
4. The Minute After Pill™ Oral Contraceptive
5. OxyMoron™
6. noMopain
7. Oil of Elixir Cream Ointment Enhancer
8. Valley of Midoll's Anti-Cramp Capsules
9. No Sweat M'Lady Deodorant
10. Texas Hold'em Hairspray
11. Preparation K
12. PeptAbysmal
13. Out Like a Lite Nighttime Sleep Aid
14. Hugh Mongo's Hair Embiggener
15. Bull Moose Elbow Salve
16. Crust Toothpaste
17. HunkaGunk Earwax Remover
18. Fungus B-Gon
19. Nick's Napalm Rub
20. Ragin' Roids (steroids from The Strong Arm of the Ma)
21. Notoriously B.I.G. Volumizing Shampoo
22. Your Gums' Best Chums Dental Floss
23. Sky High Blue Hair Dye #56
24. Snore-No-More Nose Candies

TALES TORN FROM THE HEART OF SPRINGFIELD

The Secret Life of Homer's Wife

NOW HERE'S A "NOVEL" APPROACH TO ROMANCE! ⁑TEE HEE⁑

THE FOLLOWING TUESDAY, I COULD HARDLY WAIT TO DROP MAGGIE OFF AT DAYCARE AND RUSH OVER TO MY VERY FIRST MEETING OF THE SOPHISTICATED LADIES BOOK CLUB!

ANXIOUS TO MAKE A GOOD IMPRESSION, I PREPARED A PLATTER OF MY SPECIAL HORS D'OEUVRES.

I DON'T CARE *HOW* SOPHISTICATED YOU ARE...WHO DOESN'T *LOVE* PIGS-IN-A-BLANKET?!

HELLO, RUTH! HOPE I'M NOT TOO EARLY. I'M JUST SO TICKLED PINK TO BE A MEMBER OF THE BOOK CLUB, I COULDN'T *WAIT* TO COME OVER!

YOU'RE RIGHT ON TIME, HONEY...

...STU, POUR MARGE A MARTINI!

NOTHING COULD HAVE PREPARED ME FOR THE SHOCKING SCENE OF UTTER DEPRAVITY THAT UNFOLDED BEFORE MY EYES...

DISCO STU SAYS, "SHAKE IT, BUT DON'T BREAK IT!" ONE MARTOONI IN THE AFTERNOONY COMING UP!

BETTER MAKE IT A DOUBLE, STU. SHE LOOKS LIKE SHE'S IN SHOCK.

BUT...BUT ISN'T THIS A MEETING OF THE *BOOK CLUB*?!

DON'T ASK ME, MIDGE...I'M JUST HERE FOR THE BOOZE AND BROADS.

GOODNESS GRACIOUS! I HAD UNWITTINGLY STUMBLED INTO A REAL, LIVE *SUBURBAN MAKE-OUT PARTY*! THE BOOK CLUB WAS JUST A COVER FOR A *SWINGING HOUSEWIVES CLUB*!

TO BE CONTINUED...

Repurposing Leftovers

1) Don't let your meatloaf loaf! Meatloaf is one of the most versatile leftovers around. Use an ice cream scoop to make it into meatballs! Use some scissors and cut it into letters to teach the baby how to read! Cut the loaf into small pieces and boil it up in a soup that's two parts mustard, one part ketchup! Hollow it out and serve up some chowder to put those ordinary bread bowls to shame!

2) Always keep the carcass! Whether it's turkey, chicken, or cow, always save the bones! Bones = BROTH and with the wondrous power of broth, ANYTHING can be made into soup! You should always have at least one gallon at the ready in your freezer. I once made one of Homer's favorite stews from frozen broth, half a bucket of chicken, a three-day old calzone, some parsley, and four chunks of sweet and sour pork!

3) Disguise the fries! French fries are the most reuse-iest food in your fridge! Mash 'em, hash 'em, knish 'em, or just hot dish 'em—anything you do to a potato, you can do to fries! French fries can also be used in place of **pasta!** Fries Alfredo anyone? Or... **bread!** Who wants a PB, J, & FF? How about **stuffing!** On Thanksgiving, be thankful for leftover fries baked for hours in a turkey cavity with celery and a dash of salt and pepper! **Sushi rice!** Supersize your sashimi! **Waffles!** Stick 'em together with peanut butter and slather 'em with syrup—your family won't know the difference!

for Fun and Budgetary Concerns!

4) Hot sauce brings food back to life...or hides the fact that it's dead! Whenever I'm in the Little Tijuana section of Springfield, I always stop by Mouth Blasters for a few bottles of their most powerful hot sauce. The hotter the sauce, the longer a leftover can be "left over." If I have a piece of salmon from a few days ago that's nearing the point of no return, nothing can bring it back like the power of poblano peppers!

5) Bring it to the blender and consider it a sauce! Whether it be Salisbury steak, fried shrimp, or peas and carrots, you can use it the day after by simply frappéing them up, adding some spices and tomato sauce, and serving them on top of noodles!

6) Anything can be sandwiched! No matter what the leftover, putting it between two pieces of bread with a piece of American cheese makes it into a brand-new meal!

7) When all fails, deep-fry it! I hold this truth to be self-evident in American kitchens, ANYTHING rolled in flour and plunged in hot oil is delicious, whether it's last week's pot roast or last night's Brussels sprouts! "If you fry it, they will 'yum!'"

STARK IMAGES OF A TEENAGE SHUTTERBUG

BY MARGE BOUVIER, HIGH SCHOOL PHOTOGRAPHER

LOOK OUT, ANNIE LEIBOVITZ! I'M ROCKIN' 'N' ROLLIN' AND AIMIN' 'N' SHOOTIN' AT THE LUNCHTIME

BATTLE OF THE BANDS

IN THE SCHOOL'S MULTIPURPOSE ROOM!

FIREMEN WERE CALLED TO THE SCENE OF THE **SENIOR BONFIRE** WHEN FLAMES ENGULFED PRINCIPAL DONDELINGER'S **AMC PACER.**

CHUG-A-LUGGING ROOT BEERS ON GRADUATION DAY. JUST THINK: THIS COULD BE THE LAST TIME EVER THAT HOMER & BARNEY CLINK COLD, FROSTY MUGS TOGETHER!

HOMER COULDN'T GET HIS DIPLOMA UNTIL HE PAID ALL HIS LIBRARY FINES. BUT HERE'S THE HALL PASS HE GOT SO HE COULD VISIT THE BOYS' ROOM ONE LAST TIME.

THIS IS MY MOST FAMOUS PHOTOGRAPH.

THAT'S ARTIE ZIFF GIVING A KISS TO A SURPRISED COED ON

V-J DAY

(V-NECK SWEATERS & JEANS DAY).

HOMER ASSISTS VICE-PRINCIPAL CHALMERS IN DEMONSTRATING THE CORRECT APPLICATION OF THE **BOARD OF EDUCATION.**

MRS. BUTTERWORTHY, SPRINGFIELD HIGH'S PROFESSOR OF DOMESTIC ENGINEERING. TODAY'S LESSON IS: "THE EXTRA INGREDIENT IS WORRY."

THE TEAM SPIRIT IS WILLING, BUT THE SPELLING IS WEAK.

THE DRAMA CLUB EXPLORES TEEN TOPICS IN **WAITING FOR GODOT.**

FUTURE GYM TEACHERS OF AMERICA

THE FUTURE GYM TEACHERS OF AMERICA CLUB BECAME WILDLY POPULAR AFTER EVERYONE FOUND OUT ITS MEMBERS WERE EXCUSED FROM PHYS-ED CLASS.

I TOOK THIS SELF-PORTRAIT IN THE MIRROR OF THE GIRL'S LOCKER ROOM.

PORTRAIT OF PATTY AND SELMA'S GRADUATION FROM TRAFFIC SCHOOL. TAKEN DURING MY GRIM DIANE ARBUS PERIOD.

WITH BRIGHT SHINING FACES

A selection of illuminating portraits from the Marge Simpson Picture Gallery

ARRANGEMENT IN PERIWINKLE AND RAW UMBER: PORTRAIT OF THE ARTIST'S MOTHER
Subject: Jacqueline Bouvier
Crayon on drywall

One of my earliest works. Selma managed to capture it on film before I was made to wash it off the living room wall. Suffering greatly for my art, I was then sent to my room without dinner. ▼

A LIVERPOOL LAD ▶
Subject: Ringo Starr
Ballpoint pen on ruled notebook paper
This is an initial sketch of my fave, fab drummer boy done during my Beatlemaniac period. The final version hangs in Mr. Starr's castle on the Thames!

BALD ADONIS ▲
Subject: Homer Simpson
Latex on cardboard
I won first prize at the Springfield Art Fair with this haunting, enigmatic portrait of my husband asleep in his underwear, perchance dreaming of his wife's pork chops.

THE FULL MONTY BURNS ▶
Subject: Montgomery Burns
Oil on canvas
Though I hated to admit it at the time, Mr. Burns' inspirational words, "Shut up and paint!" were just the encouragement I needed.

CENSORED

A MAN, A PLAN: NAPLANAMA!
Subject: Jebediah Obadiah Zachariah Jedediah Springfield
Ink jet print on plain paper
This was a design I submitted to the U.S. Postmaster General for consideration in the U.S. Postal Service's "America's Founding Fathers Paternity Test" commemorative postage stamp series. I'm still waiting for a reply to come in the mail. ▼

WHO'S YOUR DADDY, SPRINGFIELD?

Jebediah Obadiah Zachariah Jedediah Springfield

42 USA

▲ MY OWN-A LISA
Subject: Lisa Simpson
Felt pen on paper towel
I know da Vinci's painting is the most famous one in the world, but I honestly don't see what the big mystery is all about. What gal has a big, cheerful smile when wearing such a drab outfit?

◄ THE TEARS OF A CLOWN
Subject: Krusty the Clown
Oil on black velvet
Inspired by the lugubrious art stylings of Red Skelton, this is my attempt to show the façade behind the façade of a beloved entertainer.

SELF-PORTRAIT WITH ►
BANDAGED EAR
Subject: Marge Simpson
Oil on canvas tote bag
This was done after a rather unpleasant incident while shopping at It's a Wonderful Knife at the Squidport.

The Springfield Prison Women's Auxiliary Dinner Theatre

presents

I Never Told You "I Told You So!"

A One-Woman Musical Show
starring
MARGE SIMPSON

Book by
MARGE SIMPSON

Music by
LISA SIMPSON

Lyrics by
MARGE SIMPSON

Based on a Remark Made by
MARGE SIMPSON to HOMER SIMPSON

Costumes, Scenery, and Cast Party Favors Designed by
The Springfield Community College Extension Center

Under the Artistic Direction of
PROFESSOR LOMBARDO

Mrs. Simpson's hairstyles by
HAIRY SHEARERS

Directed by
LLEWELYN SINCLAIR
Off-Interstate 95 Drama Award™ Nominee for
Most Excruciating Performance to Watch

Who's Who in the Cast

MARGE SIMPSON made her singing debut as Blanche Dubois in Springfield Community Center's production of "Oh! Streetcar." Her past dramatic performances include a big scene she made at Hailstone's when they overcharged her for vacuum cleaner bags. She thanks her husband, Homer, and children Bart, Lisa, and Maggie. Oh, and she thanks God, too.

Musical Numbers

Act I
Overture
"Have I Ever Told You 'I Told You So!'?"
"I'm Not So Sure That's a Good Idea"
"Maybe We Should Stop and Ask for Directions"
"Don't You Think You've Had Enough to Drink?"
"Better Wait Till It Cools Before You Take a Bite"

Act II
"I Don't Think Those Are the Edible Kind"
"Careful! That Paint Is Still Wet"
"I Say We Call a Professional Electrician"
"Are You Sure You Turned the Power Off?"
"See?"

The Springfield Prison Women's Auxiliary Dinner Theatre
Maximum entertainment. Minimum security.

The Critic's Choice Remarks about

I Never Told You "I Told You So!"

"'I Never Told You "I Told You So!"' is a bittersweet musical about a wife sweetly cataloging all her bitter resentments about her husband. Its touchy-feely-sticky sentiment and a show-prolonging performance by Marge Simpson give it the piquancy of freshly cut cheese."
— *The Springfield Shopper*

"If any one woman has a reason to mount a one-woman show about what a dunderhead her husband is, Marge Simpson is that one woman."
— *MISSUS, The Little Magazine for the Little Mrs.*

"Marge Simpson gave a performance of remarkable endurance, serving up a smorgasbord of perturbed umbrage for a grueling 98½ minutes. Unfortunately, we were exhausted long before Ms. Simpson was."
— *Drama and Greg Weekly*

"…and although the audience, thankful that the ordeal was over, applauded wildly at the end of the first number, Marge Simpson, displaying a wanton disregard for the grave risk she posed to all within earshot, went on to wring the holy bejeezus out of nine more songs."
— **Kent Brockman,** *Eye on Springfield*

For complaints about our convicted waitresses spitting in your food, contact the Women's Prison Hot Line: 1-800-IMA-RATT.

¿GASP!¿ MRS. **KRABAPPEL!** SHOULDN'T YOU BE AT SCHOOL?

RELAX, MRS. SIMPSON. THE CHILDREN ARE ON AN UNSUPERVISED FIELD TRIP TO THE SCISSORS FACTORY.

IS THERE NO ONE HERE WITH ANY SHRED OF RESPECTABILITY? ARE YOU ALL SO WICKED AND DEBASED THAT YOU'VE LOST ALL SENSE OF MORAL DECENCY?!

YE-E-E-ES!

¿BOO HOO!¿ HOW COULD I HAVE BEEN SO BLIND? I'M SO ASHAMED!

THAT NIGHT, AS I CONFESSED THE ENTIRE UGLY EPISODE TO MY HUSBAND, I WAS SO AFRAID HE WOULD TURN AWAY FROM ME IN CONTEMPT. BUT HE ONLY HELD ME CLOSER IN HIS FORGIVING ARMS!

I VOWED I WOULD NEVER READ ANOTHER BOOK AGAIN!

OH, HOMER! I FEEL SO RELIEVED NOW THAT I'VE TOLD YOU EVERYTHING ABOUT THAT VILE, CONTEMPTIBLE SWINGERS' CLUB.

WELL, NOT QUITE **EVERYTHING**, MARGE... WERE THERE ANY OF THOSE LITTLE **PIGGIES-UNDER-THE-BLANKETS** HORSE DERVIES LEFT OVER?

THE END

Tips for Getting Your Family Up

MARGE'S HOUSEHOLD HELPERS

1) Make home less homey! In summer, turn up the thermostat; in winter, turn up the AC! Boil cabbage overnight! Play dental drill and brake repair sound effects CDs! Put C-SPAN or "7th Heaven" on the TV and "lose" the remote! Let a vole loose in your house! Your family will seek sanctuary in the nearest sanctuary in no time!

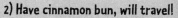

Dr. Wolfe's Greatest (Drill) Bits: Ten Root Canals.

2) Have cinnamon bun, will travel! Whip up a wonderful breakfast with all your family's favorites...and have it waiting for them in the car! When they sit down to eat, put the pedal to the metal!

3) Get them there with guilt! Use the power Jews and Catholics have been harnessing for centuries! Here are a few effective, guilt-laden phrases: "It always makes me so happy to see us all sitting in the pew together, but I guess I can just picture it in my head instead...," "I told Reverend Lovejoy we'd all be there. He's going to think I'm a liar now. Oh, well...," "God does so much for all of us...but you go ahead and sleep."

and at 'em for Church on Sunday Morning!

(Also works for mosques and synagogues!)

4) Make your family believe Sunday is Monday! Play a videotape of Monday morning TV programming on the set and get the family up and ready for the work week! Instead of dropping them off at jobs or school, take them to church and announce it's still the weekend! Cry with joy and pretend it's a miracle! If you're lucky, your family will be so happy, they'll gladly go to services!

5) Disguise the church! Use curtains, cardboard, and empty paper towel tubes to make the church look like a pony ranch, bowlatorium, or a suspiciously clean KrustyBurger restaurant! WARNING: It's best to get permission from your priest, pastor, or rabbi first. In my case, Reverend Lovejoy thought it was such a good idea he actually paid for the supplies.

6) Consider chloroform! By putting your family into a deep, chemically induced sleep, you can safely re-dress them for church and have a moving company place them in the pews before anyone arrives! And the best part: no bickering from the kids! Bring a bib, though: there will be drooling.

7) If all else fails, convert! There are plenty of exciting religions out there that utilize things like spaceships, secret underwear, and pancakes made out of potatoes! If your family won't get bright-eyed and bushy-tailed for your current faith, sit them down and find out what will get them out of bed and into a house of worship on Sunday! (Or whatever day your new, crazy religion worships on!)

NOW AT A NEWSSTAND NEAR YOU!

Pick one up today... and then be sure and wash your hands, because probably a thousand people touched it and it's sure to be covered with germs.

FRETFUL MOTHER

The Magazine for Queasy-Minded Moms

100 Everyday Childhood Safety **Pitfalls** most OVERLOOKED by CARELESS MOTHERS like **YOU!**

...ND ...RITY: Our Guide to the Top Ten **HOUSEHOLD HAZARDS** that **YOU'RE** not **WORRYING** about **ENOUGH!**

What if... **1,001** HORRIFYING **THINGS** that **COULD HAPPEN** that **YOU** never even thought about before **NOW!**

Free-Floating Anxiety:
Is it right for *YOU*? Take our quiz!

You Decide!

ARE YOU DOING ALL YOU CAN

The S.N.U.H. Newsletter

Springfieldians for Nonviolence, Understanding, and Helping

"Show them what one screwball can do!"

A Letter from our Founder:

What's SNUH with You?

Hello, Fellow Springfielders,

I have become quite concerned about the efforts made by some SNUH-zers to use this organization as an outlet for their own petty grievances. I realize that many among us are high-strung by nature and maybe even a little teeny bit oversensitive. But honestly, how a person could find it objectionable that cats and dogs run around naked is beyond me.

Nonviolently yours,
Marge Simpson

LIST OF BANNED CARTOONS

"Die! Die! You Dirty Rat Bastard!"
"Axe the Expert"
"Feline Groovy"
"Cat Got Your Tongue?"
"You 'n' Me 'n' TNT"
"It's Raining Pianos!"
"Deader Than a Doornail"
"Flatter Than a Pancake"
"Kitty Goes to Killville"

"Kitty Goes Ka-Boom"
"I Love the Knife Life"
"Dismembers Only"
"Napalm-meown Dynamite"
"The Ungrateful Dead"
"Blown to Itsy Bitsy Bits"
"Tail or No Tail"
"Slice and Dice Mice"
"Gutbusters"

PULLING THE PLUG

HOW I LEARNED TO LIVE WITHOUT TELEVISION, VIDEO GAMES, OR THE INTERNET

Editor's note: The writer we hired to write this entry suffered a complete psychotic meltdown and is currently, and ironically, undergoing electroshock treatment at Calmwood Mental Hospital. This article will be presented in the revised edition of the S.N.U.H. Newsletter.

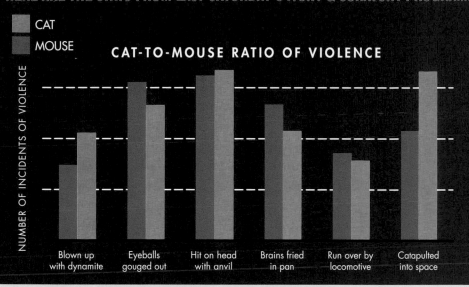

CAT

MOUSE

CAT-TO-MOUSE RATIO OF VIOLENCE

NUMBER OF INCIDENTS OF VIOLENCE

| Blown up with dynamite | Eyeballs gouged out | Hit on head with anvil | Brains fried in pan | Run over by locomotive | Catapulted into space |

Clip and send to your Congressman/lady:

---✂---

The Honorable _____
United States House of Representatives
Washington, D.C.

Dear Congressman or Congresslady,

I know you have a lot more important things to nitpick over than the senseless violence in kids' cartoon shows, but I believe the children of today will grow up to be the grown-ups of tomorrow.

And so I call on Congress to pass a constitutional amendment banning depraved acts of cat-on-mouse and mouse- on-cat violence along with a ban on the equally depraved notion of cat-on-mouse/mouse-on-cat marriage.

Thank you and have a nice recess.

Yours truly,
(your name here)
United States Citizen

Where are our children getting these violent ideas from?

- The History Network 7%
- Psychotically Violent Cartoon Studios, Inc. 6%
- Scratchy 8%
- Itchy 8%
- Bart 9%
- Mommy and Daddy 11%
- Wyle E. Coyote 1%
- Just making stuff up 14%
- Fox News 36%

Pie chart values: 36%, 6%, 7%, 8%, 8%, 9%, 11%, 1%, 14%

METHODS TO OUR MADNESS

BOYCOTT - Don't shop till they stop.

CIVIL DISOBEDIENCE - Just remember, the accent is on the first word.

DEMONSTRATIONS - These can include how-to gatherings, such as Tupperware parties and quilting bees.

FASTING - Don't try this one on an empty stomach.

MASS MARCH - Be sure to keep things moving, otherwise it's loitering with intent.

MORAL SUASION - Appealing to the moral beliefs of your opponent (not applicable in the entertainment industry).

NONCOOPERATION - I learned this one from my son, the expert.

PASSIVE RESISTANCE - This one is a lot more work than it sounds.

PETITIONS - I've found that people will sign just about anything to get past you and into Sprawl-Mart.

PICKETING - This is a lot like a mass march, only you hold signs and walk in circles.

SIT-IN – Don't try this one at home; it has absolutely no impact that way.

STRIKE - Organized withholding of something that the other side needs and can't do themselves, such as picking up garbage or writing TV shows.

VIGILS - This is a lot like picketing, only with candles instead of signs and sad faces instead of angry ones.

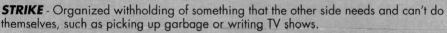

OTHER NEWSLETTERS AVAILABLE:

SPCCA
The Society for the Prevention of Cruelty to Cartoon Animals

FATCAMP
Folks Adverse to Cat and Mouse Pugnacity

LOWBLOW
League of Women Bowlers Lambasting Offensive Words

CATNGAWS
Citizens Against Their Neighbors Getting Away with Something

IOTA
Individuals Opposed to Acronyms

PWAJPFUWE
People Who Are Just Plain Fed Up with Everything

Published by
Power to the People's Pet Peeves Press

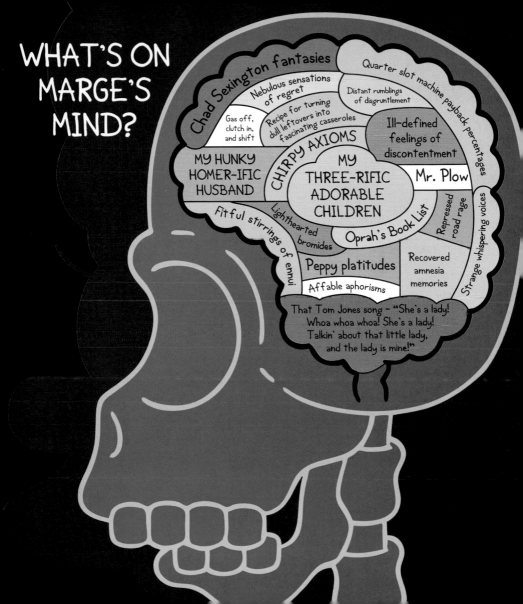

MARGE'S H.I.T.* LIST

*Horribly Imprudent Toys

WELCOME TO THE *FRIGHTENING WORLD OF TOYS!* AS A MOTHER OF THREE AND A WIFE OF ONE, I AM WELL AWARE OF HOW *UNSCRUPULOUS* MANUFACTURERS OF UNSAFE PRODUCTS PREY UPON *CHILDLIKE MINDS. SO,* IN MY CRUSADE AGAINST *ALL THINGS FRETFUL,* I'VE PUT TOGETHER THIS LIST OF TOYS THAT ARE *FORBIDDEN* IN THE SIMPSON HOUSE.

KAP'N KRUSTY'S®
LAWN HARPOONS
"Avast thar, lawn lubbers!"

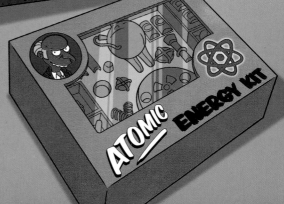

Let's Glow!
MONTY BURNS'
ATOMIC ENERGY KIT FOR KIDS™
Hours of Fissionable Fun!

UNCLE SAM'S
SLIPPERY SLOPE
BACKYARD WATER BOARD
Makes near-drowning FUN again!

LEADONARDO DA VINCI'S
LEAD-BASED PAINT-BY-NUMBERS
GIANT MURAL KIT

FIREHOUSE
PUPPY BRAND®
FLAMMABLE PJs

THE GAG GIFT THAT
REALLY MAKES 'EM GAG!
TEAR GAS CUSHION
Laugh! Cry! Choke! Puke!

ONE-EYED JACK'S
POINTY PIRATE SWORD

G.I. JOHN
*ACTION FIGURE ACCESSORY
BUTANE-FUELED LONG-RANGE
FLAMETHROWER*

PROFESSOR FRINK'S
*TOXIC CHEMICAL LAB™
101 Mind-Expanding,
Life-Shortening Experiments!*

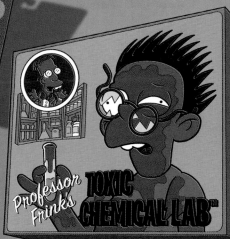

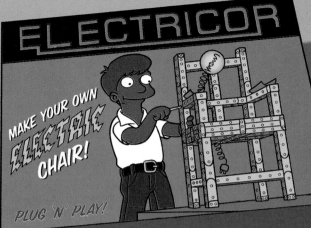

ELECTRICOR
ELECTRIC CHAIR SET
Just plug 'n' play!

GAGGY BEAR®
CHEWY CHOKABLES
*See back of package for
handy Heimlich maneuver instructions!*

UNCLE KRUSTY'S®
BEDBUG FARM
Sleep Tight! Let 'em Bite!

CHIXFLIX

Marge Simpson's Sisterhood of DVDs

THE ENGLISH PATIENT'S SPONGE BATH

The Way We Was

Like a Bat Out of Africa

Waiting for My Ex to Inhale

THE FRENCH LIEUTENANT'S WIFE'S SISTER'S NEXT DOOR NEIGHBOR

BURGER AND FRIES *TO GO* AT TIFFANY'S

YOU'VE GOT SPAM

TO, LIKE, HAVE AND TO, LIKE, SO NOT HAVE

An Officer and a Gentleman's Big Fat Greek Civil Union Ceremony

FOUR WEDDINGS, A FUNERAL, AND THEN SWING BY THE DRY CLEANER'S

While You Were Sleeping in Seattle

Stolen Magnolias

When Harry and Sally Met Thelma and Louise

A Room with a View of the Vending Machine

Breaking Wind

Lord of the Engagement Rings

My Best Friend's Wedding Planner

When a Woman Loves a Chocolate Bar

PRETTY HOOKER

The Godmother, Part II

How the Grinch Stole Stella's Groove

DEADBEAT BRIDE

RED BLAZER

COOKIE KWAN

5,800 SQUARE FEET OF SMUGNESS AWAITS YOU ON THE WEST SIDE!

Discover the essence of living in springfield's most desirable neighborhood with a luxurious house you can rub your friends' noses in! Here's your opportunity to own a home custom-designed to make guests feel small and ashamed! Enjoy room after room of unused living space! Sweeping views of all those crappy homes on the east side.

#1 ON THE WEST SIDE!

GIL GUNDERSON

NO OFFER TOO LOW. PLEASE...MAKE AN OFFER. YOU GOT AN OFFER? I NEED AN OFFER!

RUSTIC CHARMER!

The world is at your doorstep in this cozy little cottage located next to the Michael Jackson Expressway. Breezy walk-thru screen door provides easy access to nearby liquor store and 24-hr. bail bonds. Unique skyhole brightens kitchen during daylight hours. Detached bathroom. Chain link fencing indoors and out. Front lawn easily accommodates up to 4 junk cars.

REALTY

GARAGE MAHAL LUXURY ESTATES

"A commitment to excellence far beyond your own boorish personal tastes."

Reservations are being taken for Garage Mahal Luxury Estates, now under construction. 12,650 sq. ft. unaffordable homes at prices starting from $6,799,900.

Enjoy breathtaking views of Springfield's endangered wetlands!* Why live the reality when you can live the dream!
No money down, 300% financing, interest-only loans available!
Sounds too good to be true? You bet it is!

*Future site of Garage Mahal: Phase II.

NICK CALLAHAN

EXCLUSIVE AGENT FOR GARAGE MAHAL LUXURY ESTATES

CUTE LITTLE STARTER HOME!
(And by "little" I mean small. Really, really small.)

Recently Renovated Kitchen! (But still kind of cramped, if you ask me.)
Convenient Location to Shops and Restaurants! (But awfully close to a very busy, very noisy high-traffic route.) **New Paint and New Carpeting Throughout!** (That's nice, but you've got to wonder if there's something they're trying to hide.) **Come Take a Look!**
(And be sure and bring a home inspector with you, because I'm not so sure the electrical wiring is up to code.)

MARGE SIMPSON

A HOME BUYER'S BEST FRIEND!

From Lisa

A sponsorship for an orphaned pony in Jackson Hole, Wyoming.

The novel "Maternal Sunshine of the Spotless Kitchen: Clean Your House Naturally" by Rainbow Schwartzbaum.

A redeemable coupon to cook Marge a raw/vegan meal.

A nine-minute sax solo entitled "The Beehive Blue #52 Blues."

From Bart

A stick that resembles Marge.

"Hard-Boiled Eggs into Eyeballs: A Super Gross Cookbook."

Half a box of "Red Hots" with an IOU for the other half.

A portrait in hamburger fixings by noted artist Milhouse.

BENDINGLY BAD BIRTHDAY GIFTS!

(and a few good ones)

From Homer

A case of "Domestic Goddess: A Perfume by Roseanne."

A "World's Coolest Mom, World's Coldest Beer" beer cozy.

A Dallas Cowboys trivet.

A case of Dennis Franz Pasta Sauce ("Discontinued, so it's a delectable collectible!").

An extra-large colander.

A Lard Lad custom cold-cast statue.

A 36" pizza with everything on it (including shrimp, which makes Marge's throat close up).

From Maggie

A silver bracelet from Tiffany's.

A subscription to the Fruit-of-the-Month Club.

An incredible mix CD.

An XXXXL bathing cap.

A mint condition, 1963 45-RPM single of "Act Naturally" by the Beatles (signed by Ringo Starr).

MARGE'S BOTTOM

1. EMPTY CALORIES.
2. MOBILE PRETZEL RETAILING.
3. PUSHY SALESPEOPLE.
4. UPHILL BATTLES.
5. DOWNHILL SKIING.
6. MOUNTAINS.
7. MOLEHILLS.
8. ILL WILL.
9. RANDOM ACTS OF MINDLESS VIOLENCE.
10. ITCHY.
11. MINDLESS ACTS OF RANDOM VIOLENCE.
12. SCRATCHY.
13. VIOLENT ACTS OF RANDOM MINDLESSNESS.
14. DUFF DAYS BEER FESTIVAL.
15. AYN RAND.
16. SHENANIGANS.
17. ELECTRIC GARAGE DOOR OPENERS.
18. MR. BURNS' GENITALIA.

40